THE ADVENTURES OF WOMWOM!

INTRODUCING WOMWOM

Simon Saffigna

"The Adventures of WomWom. "Introducing WomWom." is an introduction to a series of envirocational ® (environmental & educational) children's storybooks and multimedia products.

Our motto:
WomWom= Happy, Healthy, Caring Children

I dedicate this book to my parents, Paul and Dianne Saffigna, who nurtured and encouraged my creativity.

Based on a true story with Adrian "Addy" Jones and WomWom, a young Australian wombat.

G'day boys and girls my name is WomWom. I am a Flinders Island wombat from Australia. I lost my mum when I was just a little baby but lucky for me Farmer Addy saved me and took care of me. I live with him on his organic fruit and vegetable farm now. Every day is a new adventure for me. Are you ready to come adventuring? Ok let's go!

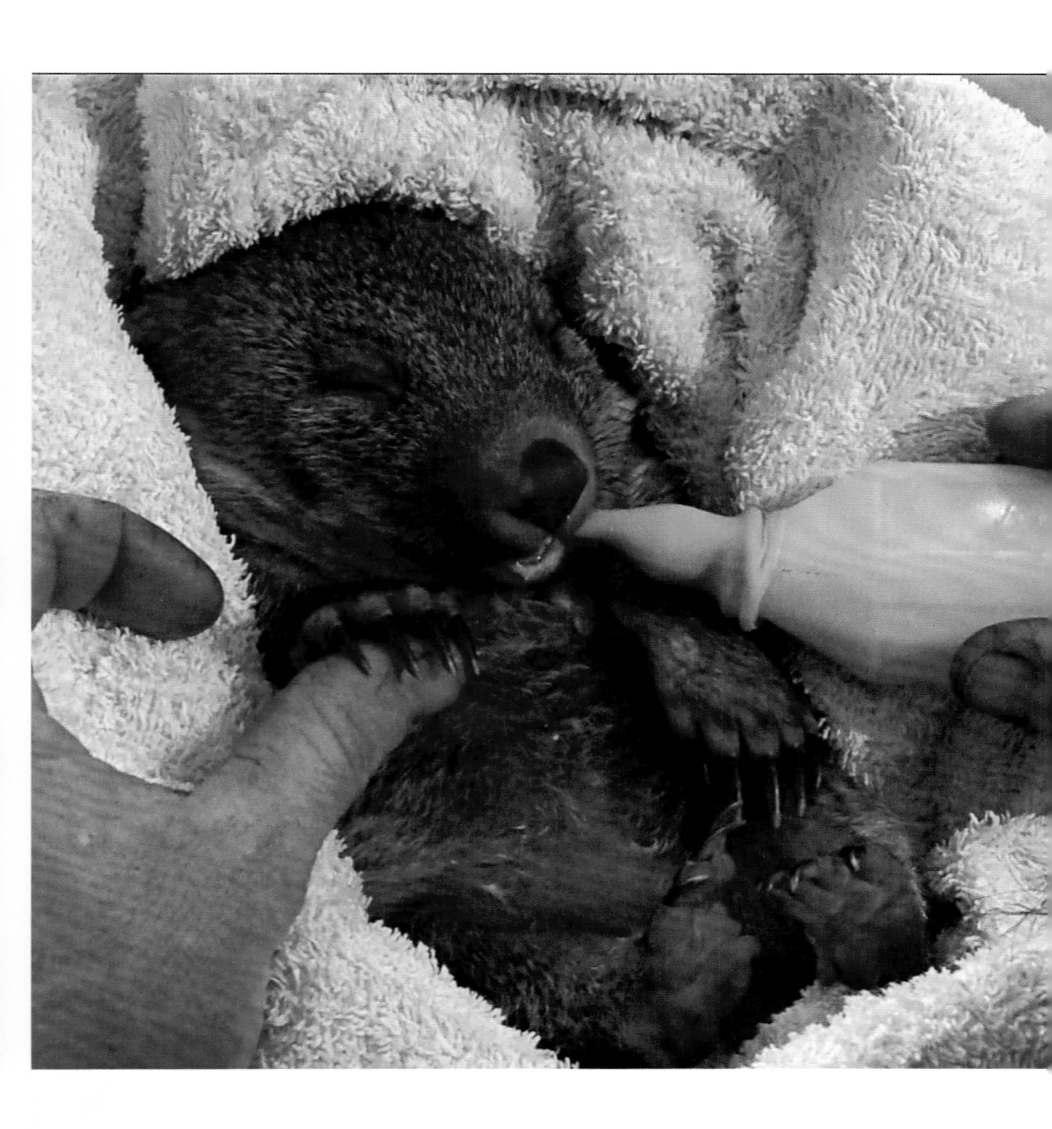

I always start the day with a healthy breakfast. It is the most important meal of the day. It gives me heaps of energy so I can adventure all day long.

Living on the farm is so much fun. There is always something cool to do. One of my favourite things to do is to help Farmer Addy in the vegetable garden.

We grow our own food on the farm. It is really important that we make sure all the plants get plenty of water and healthy plant food.

There are many different animals who live in the vegetable garden. They help to look after it. Bees are some of the most important animals in the world. They help to pollinate many of the flowering plants. This allows the food to grow.

Also there are the butterflies. They are some of the prettiest animals in the world. There are thousands of different types of butterflies. Butterflies, like the bees, are very important. They too pollinate the flowering plants.

Farmer Addy also has a worm farm. The worms eat our vegetable scraps. This makes the soil rich and allows the trees and plant life to grow big and strong - just like me.

Speaking of growing big and strong, it must be time for me to have some lunch. My friends and I eat fresh food from the garden every day.

Here are a couple of my friends now. 'Hello William the Wallaby. Hello Esta the Echidna.' They live next door in the bush, close to a creek.

Sometimes they come to visit the chickens and to eat their food too! We don't mind though. We are all friends on the farm and look after each other.

After a big lunch and adventuring all morning, I get tired and I have an afternoon sleep. Then, when I wake up again, I'm recharged and ready for more adventures. Are you ready too? Ok let's go!

Going to the beach is one of my favourite adventures. Do you like going to the beach? There is always something cool to do and many different things to see.

I like playing on the rocks and in the sand. I always see different kinds of birds at the beach. It's really important that we look after our oceans, our creeks, our rivers and all of the animals who live there.

When we go to the beach, Farmer Addy and I spend time looking at shells and collecting rubbish. Even if it is not our rubbish, by picking it up, we know it helps clean up the ocean. This means my dolphin friends and other sea life don't get tangled in it or choke on it.

Look! Here are the dolphins and there is Wilma the whale. Look how beautiful they are.

I always feel good when I know I have helped my friends, don't you?

There is no better way to end an adventurous day than by watching the sun go down at the beach and thinking about all the fun we have had. It's very, very relaxing, just like falling asleep by the fire.

Everybody needs a good night's sleep. Then we will all be ready for more adventures tomorrow. See you tomorrow boys and girls!

Suggested Follow-up Activities

Think and Talk

What is the name of the main character in the story?

What kind of an animal is WomWom?

Can you remember the names of WomWom's friends?

What important job do the bees and butterflies do?

What does pollinate mean?

Why is it important for us to pick up any rubbish on the beach and the bank of the river?

Be Creative

Draw your favourite part of the story. Don't forget to put a caption under your drawing.

Write and Illustrate

Write about an exciting adventure WomWom and Farmer Addy might have down at the beach.

GLOSSARY

P1. wombat – a furry Australian animal with very short legs, that eats plants

P1. organic – naturally grown

P6. pollinate – carry pollen from one plant to another

P6. allows – lets

P8. scraps – thrown away food

P10. couple – two

P10. wallaby – an Australian animal like a small kangaroo

P10. echidna – a spine-covered Australian animal with claws and a slender snout

P12. recharged – full of energy again

P15. tangled – caught up

P15. choke – caught in the throat

P19. adventurous – exciting

P19. relaxing – restful